# GOD
# IN THE
# MIRROR

## DISCUSSION GUIDE

# GOD
# IN THE
# MIRROR

DISCUSSION GUIDE

Discovering Who You
Were Created to Be

# MILES
# McPHERSON

with Kevin and Sherry Harney

**BakerBooks**

*a division of Baker Publishing Group*
Grand Rapids, Michigan

© 2013 by Miles McPherson

Published by Baker Books
a division of Baker Publishing Group
P.O. Box 6287, Grand Rapids, MI 49516-6287
www.bakerbooks.com

ISBN 978-0-8010-4879-1

Printed in the United States of America

Library of Congress Cataloging-in-Publication Data is on file at the Library of Congress, Washington, DC.

The internet addresses, email addresses, and phone numbers in this book are accurate at the time of publication. They are provided as a resource. Baker Publishing Group does not endorse them or vouch for their content or permanence.

13   14   15   16   17   18   19      7   6   5   4   3   2   1

# Contents

# Of Note

The quotations interspersed throughout this guide are excerpts from the DVD curriculum for *God in the Mirror* and the book *God in the Mirror* by Miles McPherson (Baker Books, 2013). All other resources—including introductions, small group questions, Looking in the Mirror activities, journal ideas, and prayer direction—have been written by Kevin and Sherry Harney in collaboration with Miles McPherson.

# A Word from Miles McPherson

I am excited about the fact that you will be learning to look in the mirror and discover that you are gazing at a masterpiece of God. In the coming weeks you will learn fresh and exciting things about God, yourself, and every person you have ever met.

The book *God in the Mirror*, this DVD, and the participant's guide that you hold in your hands will function together as a road map for this adventure of learning and life transformation. If you fully engage with your small group over the coming six sessions, I believe you will never be the same.

I invite you to enter this experience with eyes ready to see what God wants to reveal, ears open to hear what He wants to speak to you, and a life that is open and responsive to God's leading.

You were made in the very image of the God of the universe!

You are unique, wonderful, and loved more than you can imagine or dream!

As you see, accept, and seek to grow this image of God that is in you, you will discover a life of meaning, joy, adventure, and connection with God.

My prayer is that you will learn to look in the mirror and see the God who made you, loves you, and came to this earth to die for you.

As you do, I pray you will be transformed to look more and more like Jesus, so that the whole world will see, experience, and accept His amazing grace and love.

*Enjoy the journey,*

*Miles McPherson*

# OVERVIEW

*Are You Ready for This?*

## Introduction

Art represents the artist. This is true of music, sculpture, paintings, and every creative expression. When we listen to a brilliant orchestral piece, we learn something about the master composer. When we gaze on an exquisite painting, we learn about the one who brushed each stroke on the canvas. If you want to get to know an artist, simply study their work.

This is not just true of master artists but of all artists. Look at a finger painting hanging on a grandma and grandpa's refrigerator door and you will gain insight into the little granddaughter who gave it to them as a gift of love. Listen to the sounds coming out of the garage as a group of high school students practice their music with passion and ear-piercing volume and you will find a window to the souls of these young people. Study the art and you will gain understanding of the artist.

God is the ultimate and greatest of all artists. His handiwork declares His presence, creativity, glory, and imagination. A cricket chirping in the dark of the night, lifting a song to heaven; a sunset piercing the morning sky; a waterfall roaring with immeasurable power; a puppy chasing its own tail—all of these works of art point to the Master Artist. If you want to get to know God better, slow down and investigate the beauty and wonder of His art . . . it is all around you!

Strangely, the apex of God's artistic creation is often forgotten. We are quick to notice God in the power of a storm or the serenity of a sunset, but sometimes we miss God's presence in the greatest of all His creative handiwork. If you want to see the best of the best of all God has made, in the entire universe, you don't need a telescope or a microscope. What you need is a mirror.

You and I are the best reflection of the glory, beauty, and wonder of God. We were made in His image and bear His likeness. If you want to deepen your understanding of God, try this simple exercise . . . look in the mirror.

## Talk about It

What is one physical feature, habit, or mannerism that people notice in you that they say reminds them of your father, mother, or some other family member? How do you feel when someone points this out?

God designed you in His image so that when He looks at you, it'll be like He's looking into a mirror.

**Video Teaching Notes**

*As you watch the DVD teaching segment for session 1, use the following outline to record anything that stands out to you, or simply use the bullet points as reminders of what Miles talked about in this session.*

- A story of twins

- What does God expect to see when He looks at us?

- The "bling factor"

- Our "God image" (the *imago Dei*) reflects many things about our Maker

- Five facets:
  1) I

  2) M

  3) A

  4) G

  5) E

---

There is no one like you in the entire world. God made you to reflect His creative genius.

---

## DVD Discussion

1. As you think about the people in your life who reflect the image of God to you, talk about one characteristic of God you have seen displayed in this person's life and the effect it has had on you.

2. What is one characteristic of God that you see growing in your life? If people were to look closely at you, how might they get to know God better as they observe this characteristic?

3. What are some ways we can get closer to God and allow His light to shine more and more in our lives so that we can reflect His light and presence into the world around us?

---

God created us in such a way that we provide an accurate reflection of His glory back to Him and onto the world.

---

**Read** Psalm 19:1–6 and Romans 1:20

4. How does God's creation declare and proclaim His presence, power, and glory? How do you experience God when you look at and experience His creative beauty?

**Read** Psalm 8

5. What does God teach you about Himself in Psalm 8? What does He teach you about who you are in this psalm?

6. How can looking at creation reveal *one* of these attributes of God?

God is *intelligent* . . .

God is *creative* . . .

God is *patient* . . .

God is *loving* . . .

Some other attribute . . .

7. How can looking in the mirror at yourself (or looking at another person) reveal *one* of these attributes of God?

God is *intelligent* . . .

God is *creative* . . .

God is *patient* . . .

God is *wise* . . .

God is *compassionate* . . .

God is *loving* . . .

Some other attribute . . .

---

Each one of us is unique, and
we were created to provide
the most complete mirror
image of God on earth.

---

8. Miles uses a creative mnemonic (IMAGE) to help us remember
   five facets of our "God image." Which of these do you feel
   most comfortable with and what is one way you see this facet
   of God's image in you?

Facet 1- **I**  You are an **Individually Unique** person
Facet 2- **M**  You were made to be a **Moral Mirror** of God's character
Facet 3- **A**  You have been given **Authority to Rule**
Facet 4- **G**  You are **God's Friend**
Facet 5- **E**  You were created to be **Eternal**

Which of these five is hardest for you to grasp and why is this
a challenging reality for you to embrace?

9. When you think of the five facets of God's image in us as human beings, it is clear that His perfect image has been blurred because of sin. How do we experience the blurring of God's image in *one* of these facets?

Facet 1- **I**   You are an **Individually Unique** person
Facet 2- **M**   You were made to be a **Moral Mirror** of God's character
Facet 3- **A**   You have been given **Authority to Rule**
Facet 4- **G**   You are **God's Friend**
Facet 5- **E**   You were created to be **Eternal**

What is one practical way we can clear up this aspect of God's image in us and reveal a clearer picture of God to the people around us?

10. Miles teaches that it is our responsibility to "maximize God's diamond bling and let Him shine through us to the world." What is one way you can work on increasing God's "bling" in your life?

What can you do in the coming week to let God's light shine in and through you in one of the five facets explored in this session?

> Our God image is not a static
> diamond. It is active and alive!

## Closing Prayer

*Spend time in your group praying in some of the following directions:*

- Thank God for the beauty of His creative artwork all around the world, and right in your own backyard.
- Thank God that He has chosen to let His light, life, and love shine through you.
- Give praise to God for the good traits and characteristics that your earthly parents have passed on to you.
- Pray that the image of God will shine, in growing measure, through the lives of each person in your small group.
- Ask the Holy Spirit to help you notice the presence and image of God in the people you encounter each day . . . even the tough people.
- Ask God to do great things in your life and the lives of your group members as you study *God in the Mirror* as a group in the coming weeks.

> God created you to have an intimate
> and loving friendship with Him!

## Looking in the Mirror

*Take time to engage in one or more of the following exercises before your next group meeting.*

## 1. Artistic Project

Take time in the coming days to work on some kind of artistic venture. Buy a set of watercolors and paint something. Finish the scrapbook project that is in the closet. Begin singing again and write a few lines of a new tune. Cook a recipe you haven't tried before. Get out your old guitar and play a song. Sculpt something, make a piece of pottery, crochet a scarf, or engage in some other kind of artistic expression.

As you enter into this creative process, take note of how this artistic venture captures something about who you are, how you think, what you love, or some part of your character.

If you feel particularly bold, you might want to share this experience with your group the next time you meet. Introduce your art and tell them what you learned about yourself in the process of creating it.

## 2. Studying the Master Artist

Take a walk outdoors and make a list of things God has made. Reflect on what is unique about each thing and then write down what you learn about God through what you have seen. Keep a journal in the space provided.

| What God made | Why it is unique | What I learn about the Artist |
|---|---|---|
|  |  |  |
|  |  |  |
|  |  |  |

| What God made | Why it is unique | What I learn about the Artist |
| --- | --- | --- |
| | | |
| | | |
| | | |
| | | |
| | | |
| | | |
| | | |
| | | |

Take time to share something from your list with a friend and tell them what you saw and learned about God. This could be someone who knows and loves God, or even someone who is still searching spiritually.

---

We were not created to be robots,
programmed to follow a set pattern
of behaviors. We were made to
live in friendship with God.

---

### 3. Looking for God's Bling

Take time in the coming days to study the people around you. Really look to discover where the light and "bling" of God is shining through. Keep a list of your observations in the space provided.

| Name of the person | How I see God's "bling" in this person | What this teaches me about the God who made them |
|---|---|---|
|  |  |  |
|  |  |  |
|  |  |  |
|  |  |  |
|  |  |  |
|  |  |  |
|  |  |  |

| Name of the person | How I see God's "bling" in this person | What this teaches me about the God who made them |
|---|---|---|
|  |  |  |
|  |  |  |
|  |  |  |

## 4. Journal . . .

*Use the space provided below to write some reflections on the following topics:*

- How God is an artist and how I am one of His masterpieces.
- Some of the ways I see God's "bling" in the world around me, including the people in my life.
- How I can grow in each of the five areas of God's image in me.

_____

_____

_____

_____

_____

_____

_____

_____

_____

_____

_____

_____

_____

_____

_____

## Recommended Reading

As you reflect on what you have learned in this session, you may want to read the introduction in the book *God in the Mirror* by Miles McPherson.

In preparation for session 2, you may want to read part 1, chapters 1–4, of *God in the Mirror*.

# You Were Created to Be
# INDIVIDUALLY UNIQUE

## Introduction

It was graduation day at Wellesley High School in Massachusetts. The commencement speaker stood up to give the address. His message to the graduating high school students (and their parents) was not what they expected to hear. The message was so unique that it became an instant internet sensation, watched by more than 1.5 million people. The theme of his speech was not the stuff of "normal" graduation addresses.

This speaker did not say, "You can go out there and conquer the world!" He did not talk about how "special," "accomplished," or "valuable" each person was. He gave very little praise or kudos to the 2012 graduating class of Wellesley High School. Instead, the refrain through the whole speech was shocking and surprising.

His graduation talk was simply titled "You Are Not Special!"

For about twelve minutes the speaker explained why each person in that graduating class was really not that unique, special, or distinct from the rest of the high school students graduating from about 37,000 other high schools that year all over the country. He even pointed out that the most "outstanding" students in their class, their valedictorian and class president, still numbered among the other 37,000 valedictorians and class presidents around the country. He slowed down and said it again: "You are not special!"

A casual viewer of this strange graduation speech might initially think the speaker actually thought that none of these students were unique and valuable, but this was not the point of his speech at all. He was really saying that every one of the 6.8 billion people on this planet can be unique and special—if we refuse to take the easy road of conforming and following the crowd.

At the end of his speech, David McCullough Jr. says, "Then you too will discover the great and curious truth of the human experience is that selflessness is the best thing you can do for yourself. The sweetest joys of life, then, come only with the recognition that you are not special, because everyone is!"

After telling the graduating class of Wellesley High School "You are not special" over and over again, the commencement speaker went on to tell all of them that they are actually very special. He exhorted them to not conform to the society around them or follow the easy path that so many people walk. He called them to discover how unique and special all of them could be!

## Talk about It

What is one way our culture seeks to pressure us to conform and become just like everyone else rather than be the unique person God has made us to be?

Tell about a time you gave in, conformed, and later looked back and regretted that decision.

---

Our culture places so much pressure
on people to fit in and conform that
we can lose the freedom God has
given us to be uniquely creative.

---

 **Video Teaching Notes**

*As you watch the DVD teaching segment for session 2, use the following outline to record anything that stands out to you, or simply use the bullet points as reminders of what Miles talked about in this session.*

- You have global uniqueness

- The I AM factor

- People are different than the rest of creation

- You are uniquely different than all other people

- The I AM imposter

- Jesus . . . the Great I AM

---

Our "I AM factor"—our individual
uniqueness—positions us alone
above all living things to recognize,
appreciate, interpret, and interact
with God's invisible attributes.

---

## DVD Discussion

1. If one of your parents or a close friend could come and speak to your small group right now, what is one thing you think they might say is unique and wonderful about you?

2. In the DVD, Miles talks about your "global uniqueness." He says, "There is no one like you on the entire planet." What is he getting at? Do you agree or disagree . . . and defend your answer?

---

God's intention is for you to develop your full potential.

---

**Read** Psalm 139:13–16

3. When some people look in the mirror, they don't like what they see and are very self-critical. When others look in the mirror, they can be arrogant and brag on themselves. According to this passage, what does God want you to see when you look in the mirror?

How would our view of ourselves change if we saw ourselves the way God sees us?

---

## Your purpose is important, intentional, and God ordained.

---

4. According to Psalm 139, how long has God been involved in your life and what implications does this have on how you view both God and yourself?

5. If you were talking to someone who does not see their own uniqueness and the beauty of who God has made them to be, what advice would you give them? What would you tell them about who God has made them to be?

Why is it so hard to give ourselves that same advice when we look in the mirror?

**Read** Exodus 3:11–15; John 8:58–59; and Genesis 1:26–28

6. What makes God absolutely unique and different than anything in creation? How does the name I AM, in these passages, reveal God's absolute uniqueness?

7. Miles talks about how human beings are unique and designed by God to be above everything else He has made. What are some of the things that make human beings unique, special, and distinct among all of God's creation?

8. Human beings have the ability to be creative, inventive, and innovative. Tell about a way God has made you to be creative. It could be through music, dance, humor, gardening, problem-solving, writing, cooking, a craft, woodworking, engineering, and the list goes on. How does your expression of this kind of inventiveness reveal the creativity and presence of God in you?

How can this part of you reflect the I AM-ness of God to the people around you?

There's absolutely no one who can do what you can do in the way God has designed for you to do it.

**Read** John 8:42–44; 1 Peter 5:8–9; and Job 1:6–12

9. In the DVD, Miles tells us that Satan is in the business of convincing us that we should live independent of God as an I AM imposter. The enemy wants us to express our individually without God and believe we can have glory and "bling" without God. How do you see Satan influencing people to live and think this way in our world today?

How has the enemy influenced you to buy into this kind of thinking and what can you do to battle against this dangerous thinking?

---

Remember, Satan can't destroy
you without your participation.

---

**Read** Philippians 2:5–11; Colossians 1:15–20; and Hebrews 1:1–6

10. According to these passages, how is Jesus unique among all people who have lived on this earth?

11. How does having a living and powerful relationship with Jesus help you walk away from your I AM imposter and toward surrender to the Great I AM?

What is one practical action you can take in the coming days to walk away from being an I AM imposter and embrace who you are made to be in Jesus? How can your group members pray for you and cheer you on as you take this step?

> The only way God is going to see Himself in us on this side of heaven is if He Himself lives in us.

## Closing Prayer

*Spend time in your group praying in some of the following directions:*

- Thank God for how He has made each of us unique from the rest of His creation.
- Acknowledge before God that He has made you special and different than anyone else in the world.

- Praise God as the Great I AM and lift up words of celebration for how God is unique, special, powerful, and glorious above all else in the universe.
- Invite God to help you see His image in you and to learn how to celebrate the I AM factor that He has placed in you and wants to grow in you.
- Confess and admit where you have become an I AM imposter and ask God to help you walk in His power and never your own.
- Celebrate Jesus as the I AM who entered history and showed us how to live and love in a way that honors God. Pray for power to be more and more like Jesus.

My prayer is that God opens
your eyes and reveals to you who
you are and where your life is
going so you will not allow it to
be destroyed by Satan's lies.

## Looking in the Mirror

*Take time to engage in one or more of the following exercises before your next group meeting.*

### 1. YouTube Sensation

Watch the commencement speech "You Are Not Special" on YouTube. What messages in the video are helpful and where does this speaker get it wrong? Just do a search on YouTube with the words "Commencement You Are Not Special."

## 2. Look in the Mirror

Read Psalm 139. Let this passage become a mirror to reflect what God teaches about Himself and about you. Reflect on what you learn about God. How does He love you, interact with you, and invest in your life? What do you learn about the way God sees you and all of the people He has made. How should this influence how you view yourself and treat the people around you?

What do I learn about God in this psalm?

What do I learn about how God sees me?

How should the message of this psalm impact the way I view other people?

---

We're spiritual beings having a
human experience, not human beings
having a spiritual experience.

---

### 3. What Makes Me Unique

Take time to make a short list of some of the things that make you unique. Write these down as a celebration of God's amazing craftsmanship, creativity, and love for diversity.

God has made me unique **physically** in the way He has made my . . .

God has made me unique in my **abilities** . . .

God has made me unique **spiritually** because . . .

God has made me unique in my **attitudes** and outlook because I . . .

### 4. Restoration Project

Identify an area of your life where the enemy has gotten you to buy into the I AM imposter deception. How have you been drawn into believing in your own glory, "bling," and abilities, but forgotten that all of these are a gift and reflection of God's goodness?

What can you do to submit this specific area of your life back to God's leadership? How can you confess this area of sin and invite God to return as the Great I AM over this area of your life?

What specific action can you take in the next twenty-four hours and the next week to begin making a change in this area of your life?

## 5. Journal . . .

*Use the space provided below to write some reflections on the following topics:*

- Read Psalm 139 and write down some of the things you learn about who God has made you to be. Take note of who God is as the creator and maker of all people.
- What are some of the unique things about how you look, act, and respond to life that you have tried to cover up, get rid of, or ignore? How can you embrace the unique ways God has made you?
- Write prayers of thanks for the things that are unique about the people close to you. Pray for them to embrace who God has made them to be.
- Confess where you are tempted to become an I AM imposter. Ask God to help you avoid the folly of relying on your own strength.

## Individually Unique

_____

_____

_____

_____

_____

_____

_____

_____

_____

_____

_____

_____

## Recommended Reading

In preparation for session 3, you may want to read part 2, chapters 5–8, of the book *God in the Mirror*.

# You Were Created to Be
# GOD'S MORAL MIRROR

## Introduction

Have you ever watched kids play a game together? Or, more specifically, have you watched kids play a game where they were not really sure of the rules? The debates begin right away and the game becomes a series of arguments or even fights. The kids try to make things up as they go and negotiate a set of rules that will favor—you guessed it—themselves. This leads to a game that is no fun and maybe even to the splintering of fragile friendships.

It is very different when everyone knows the rules and agrees to follow them. Kids can be playing Monopoly, touch football, or Simon Says, and if they all know and agree on the rules, the game is fun. There might be an occasional argument over a minor area of disagreement, but the rules actually bring order and make the game enjoyable. Rules keep the game from becoming a war zone.

In our culture we are seeing a generation of people growing up believing there are no boundaries or rules when it comes to morality.

They have never read the instructions (the Bible), or they simply ignore what God has to say about the best way for us to live our lives. This leads to confusion, fighting, and countless hurts and broken hearts. God made us, He invented life, and He knows the best way for us to live. When we follow His moral guidelines and plan, life becomes fun, joyful, and safer for everyone.

## Talk about It

Tell about a time when you saw kids (or maybe adults) debating and arguing about the rules to a game. When there was confusion about the rules and boundaries, how did this impact the enjoyment of the game?

> If there's no absolute moral standard, then no one has a basis for determining good and evil.

##  Video Teaching Notes

*As you watch the DVD teaching segment for session 3, use the following outline to record anything that stands out to you, or simply use the bullet points as reminders of what Miles talked about in this session.*

- You were made to reflect God's light

- Reflecting God's morality

- Natural light . . . the I AM imposter (all about me)

- Spiritual light . . . the I AM factor (all about God)

- Invite Jesus—Mr. Integrity—in!

---

As moral mirrors, we don't have any
holiness of our own; we have to
rely on God to provide His holiness
for our moral mirror to reflect.

---

## DVD Discussion

1. Tell about a time you saw a Christian truly glow with the presence of God in their heart and life. What was it that you saw in this person that made them radiant with the presence of God?

2. How has our culture's understanding of what is "moral and right" changed in the past couple of decades?

   How have some of these changes in the rules, according to society, impacted the church and Christians in this generation?

   Some things are simply right and
   some things are simply wrong—
   all the time, everywhere.

3. In the DVD, Miles gives this challenge: "May your morality be a reflection of God's morality and may your right and wrong

be a mirror of God's right and wrong." How might our lives change if we really embraced this challenge every day?

How might Christians impact culture in new and powerful ways if we lived out this challenge Miles puts before us?

4. What are some of God's moral absolutes that never change? How can these serve as an anchor that brings hope and security in a very fluid world?

---

God's moral guidelines never change; they're timeless—the same yesterday, today, and tomorrow, and forever (Heb. 13:8).

---

5. *Natural light* is what we think is right in our own eyes and what is seen as right in the eyes of other people. This is all about what pleases us and makes people look good. *Spiritual*

*light* is the light that comes from God and glorifies Him . . . it makes God look good. How can these two kinds of light look and feel similar?

What are some possible consequences if we get these two kinds of light confused?

---

Our spiritual light doesn't come from us; it is the supernatural light from Christ Himself that shines through us.

---

**Read** 1 Peter 5:8–9; John 8:44; Matthew 4:1–11; and Genesis 3:1–7
    6. What do you learn about the character and tactics of the devil from these passages?

Character:

Tactics:

How do you see Satan using many of these same tactics in our world today?

7. Natural light feeds the I AM imposter in us. Satan uses it to lure us toward his plans and away from the will of God and what is truly morally right and pure. Natural light might lead us to what is "almost right" or what is "partially right," or even what seems "culturally right," but it will never lead us to what is "perfectly and completely right" in God's sight. What are some of the battlegrounds where Satan seems to be enticing people (including some Christians) to adopt a false morality that is untrue or partially true?

How do we identify the enemy's tactics and seek to let the absolutely true moral absolutes of God's light shine into our world, society, and culture today?

Satan's goal is to remove all of
God's moral boundaries from
humanity. Imagine the chaos.
Imagine the cruelty and suffering.

**Read** 2 Timothy 3:14–17; Hebrews 4:12; Psalm 119:1–16

8. What does the Bible teach us about itself in these passages?

9. Miles teaches that knowing and obeying the Word of God is the best way to reflect the I AM spiritual light of God into our dark world. The Bible becomes the frame for the mirror of our life. Tell about how you let what the Bible teaches become the frame that guides the moral boundaries of your life.

Living consistent with God's Word
means simply obeying His Word.

10. What are some of the things that distract us or drive us away from reading, studying, and really following the moral boundaries God gives us in the Bible?

What can you do to increase your commitment to know and follow the unchanging and hope-giving teaching of God's Word?

How can your group members pray for you and keep you accountable as you increase your commitment to knowing and following the teachings of Scripture?

11. We need Mr. Integrity—Jesus—in us if we are going to shine the supernatural light of God that reflects His morality in our broken and sinful world. If you are a follower of Jesus and have invited Him into your life, tell about how your moral code has changed since you began walking with Him and following His Word.

Jesus voluntarily died for us so
we can voluntarily live for Him!

## Closing Prayer

*Spend time in your group praying in some of the following directions:*

- Thank God for His glow and light that shines into and through your life.
- Ask God to help you and the members of your small group (and your church) make a difference in your community as you reflect the moral standards of God's Word into your community and relationships.
- Pray that the light of Jesus will be seen in your life and draw other people to the Savior.
- Confess where your motives and the driving force in your life can be self-centered or based on what other people think.
- Ask the Holy Spirit to move you to actions, attitudes, and behaviors that honor God and shine His light.
- Pray that you will be able to see when you are being moved by natural light and not God's spiritual light.
- If you are a follower of Jesus, thank Him for entering your life and bringing spiritual light and a new view of morality.
- If you are not yet a follower of Jesus, consider inviting Him in and ask for His light to cleanse and guide you as you learn a new way of living.

One way we can tell our love is
perfected in Jesus is when we're
able to maintain His joy and
peace in every circumstance.

## Looking in the Mirror

*Take time to engage in one or more of the following exercises before your next group meeting.*

### 1. The Truth about My Heart

All of us can miss the mark, be moved by wrong motivation, and let natural light shine through our life for self-centered reasons. There are times when we don't even notice it. Sometimes it is healthy to take an honest look at our heart and examine what motives are driving us. Use the space below to process through an honest and faith-filled experience of self-examination.

- **Pray** for the Holy Spirit to search your heart and uncover sources of natural light that might be ignited in your life. (Read Psalm 139:1–6, 23–24.)

- **Identify** a behavior or practice in your life that looks good on the outside, but you know your motive and the driving force behind this is your own glory, or impressing others.

- **Confess** this sinful motive to God. Admit that you are not moved by bringing glory to God or pleasing Him, but that your primary driving force is to impress people, or bring recognition to yourself. Honestly confess this to the God who knows and loves you!

- **Ask** God to change your heart and motives. Invite Him to shine His light on, in, and through you.

Make this process a regular part of your prayer life. Plead with God to change your heart and motives, with each passing day, to reflect His light and bring Him praise and glory.

### 2. Natural Light and Supernatural Light

Use the list provided below to guide your reflection. Think about some of these actions or behaviors and how they can look the same on the outside, but be driven by very different motivations. Use the space provided to write down some of the motives that reveal if this action is about natural light (that places the focus on people) or spiritual light (that lifts up God).

**Feeding the Poor:**

*Natural light* (possible people-centered motives . . . including me-centered motives)—

*Spiritual light* (God-glorifying motives)—

*How does this action or behavior change when it is guided by spiritual light?*

**Going to Church:**

*Natural light* (possible people-centered motives . . . including me-centered motives)—

*Spiritual light* (God-glorifying motives)—

*How does this action or behavior change when it is guided by spiritual light?*

**Going on a Mission Trip:**

*Natural light* (possible people-centered motives . . . including me-centered motives)—

*Spiritual light* (God-glorifying motives)—

*How does this action or behavior change when it is guided by spiritual light?*

**Giving Offerings:**

*Natural light* (possible people-centered motives . . . including me-centered motives)—

*Spiritual light* (God-glorifying motives)—

*How does this action or behavior change when it is guided by spiritual light?*

**Telling People about Jesus:**

*Natural light* (possible people-centered motives . . . including me-centered motives)—

*Spiritual light* (God-glorifying motives)—

*How does this action or behavior change when it is guided by spiritual light?*

## Helping a Neighbor in a Time of Need:

*Natural light* (possible people-centered motives . . . including me-centered motives)—

*Spiritual light* (God-glorifying motives)—

*How does this action or behavior change when it is guided by spiritual light?*

## Serving at a Community Helping Event:

*Natural light* (possible people-centered motives . . . including me-centered motives)—

*Spiritual light* (God-glorifying motives)—

*How does this action or behavior change when it is guided by spiritual light?*

When Christ has complete control of
our hearts, He has control of our lives,
and only then can our lives become
mirrors of God's moral character.

*3. Journal . . .*

*Use the space provided below to write some reflections on the following topics:*

- Make a list of some of the ways people in our culture are seeking to adjust, shape, or completely change what is seen as "morally acceptable."
- How am I living in "natural light" and being motived by selfish gain or a desire to impress other people?
- How can I walk more and more in the "spiritual light" of God?
- List some of the people I love and care about who have embraced and adopted a compromised moral lifestyle . . . and how I can pray for them and challenge them to see God's great plan for their life.

_____

_____

_____

_____

_____

_____

_____

_____

_____

_____

_____

_____

_____

_____

_____

_____

## Recommended Reading

In preparation for session 4, you may want to read part 3, chapters 9–12, of the book *God in the Mirror*.

# You Were Created with the
# AUTHORITY TO RULE

## Introduction

Think back over your years in school. Can you remember your teachers? Can you close your eyes and picture a face of a memorable teacher from your past? Do you remember names of teachers from certain years of your education? Can you even remember, in vivid color and detail, encounters, conversations, or specific things they said to you?

The memory of some teachers fades with time and becomes a blur through the years. But there are teachers we will never forget. Their face is locked in our memory bank; their voice still echoes in the recesses of our mind. Our encounters with these influential authority figures are still shaping who we are today.

If we are honest, the memorable teachers from our past tend to come in two very distinct and radically different groups.

First, there were the teachers who were kind, loving, safe, and encouraging, and taught us great lessons that still influence who we are becoming today. These teachers created an environment where we felt secure, valued, and excited to learn. These heroic people took their place of authority and used it to build up children as they lavished them with kindness. Teachers like this will never be forgotten.

Second, and just as memorable, were those teachers who abused their place of authority. Their tongue was sharp and they were quick to criticize and even embarrass the kids in their class. They might have built up minds through educating, but they broke the spirits of the children under their charge with intimidation, criticism, and even antagonism. They will forever be locked in our memory, but for all the wrong reasons.

A teacher is given a certain measure of authority, and they have to decide if they will use it to build, bless, and encourage. Or they will use this unique role of authority to intimidate, discourage, and criticize. Both will be remembered, but in radically different ways.

## Talk about It

Tell about a teacher from your childhood who used their authority to build children up, show love, and make learning a joyous experience.
   *or*
Tell about a teacher in your life (without using a name) who used their place of authority to discourage children and did not build into their lives in positive ways.

God gave us His authority so we would promote the original purpose of everything He created—namely, the image of God in people.

## Video Teaching Notes

*As you watch the DVD teaching segment for session 4, use the following outline to record anything that stands out to you, or simply use the bullet points as reminders of what Miles talked about in this session.*

- In the beginning, God used His authority and power to create an environment where people could flourish and pursue His purposes.


- Our place of authority in God's creation


- Don't be an "authority taker," but use authority to unleash the potential of the people around you.


- Taking authority over ourselves . . . What does this look like?


You were created to be a main
conduit of Jesus's authority.

## DVD Discussion

1. Miles tells about how he and his wife tried to create an environment where their baby daughter Kelly would thrive, grow, and become all God wanted her to be. Tell your own story about a relationship where God gave you authority over someone and you tried to create a positive and God-honoring environment for them.

**Read** Genesis 1:1–25

2. When you look at the first chapter of the Bible, how do you see God using His power and authority to make a place, and environment, for His children to thrive and follow Him? What does this teach you about how God uses authority and how He wants us to use it?

We were created to be givers, not takers, and especially not takers of the resources for others to develop physically, emotionally and spiritually.

3. Miles teaches about how God invested great care and personal attention in how He made our world, including the animals and plant life. How do you see God's tender hand and concern for you when you look at this world, the animals He has made, and the intricacies of nature?

4. What are some specific ways we can care for God's creation, protect what He has made, and be good stewards of this world God has given us authority over?

What is one action you, or your group, can take to care for the beautiful artwork of God's world that He has provided for us?

---

It is one thing to have access
to God's authority, but quite
another to submit to it.

---

**Read** Ephesians 5:22–33

5. Some people see submission as weakness and authority as license to dominate another person. How does this passage and what Miles teaches in the DVD contradict this kind of thinking?

When God gives a person leadership, headship, or authority, what is He calling them to do with this place of responsibility?

**Read** Matthew 20:25–28

6. What are some ways people have misunderstood or abused the idea of authority or headship? Why is it critical that we understand a biblical call to servant leadership rather than a human desire for control and domination?

---

Authority takers are people who reach for either more authority than God originally intended for them, or they apply authority over things that God never intended for them to take.

---

**Read** Genesis 1:26–31 and 2:15–25

7. What do you learn about God's concern for people and the intimate and personal way He created us? What do these passages teach you about the value and dignity of each person God made and each person you meet in the course of a day?




8. The apex and crowning jewel of God's creation is not mountains, oceans, the sun and moon, or the star-filled sky. God is clear that people are the most valuable part of all He has made. Of all that we are called to steward, nurture, and care for, people come at the top of the list. Take time as a small group and make a list of at least twenty specific ways we can steward, nurture, build up, or care for the people in our lives:

Take time to talk about one or more of these ideas that you can put into action in your life in the coming week. Invite your group members to pray for you as you invest in specific relationships and learn to honor people and help them grow more into the image of Jesus.

We look at how God loves us, and
that is how we are to love ourselves.

**Read** Proverbs 12:18; 18:21; and James 3:1–12

9. What do you learn about the power of our words from these passages? Give an example of how you have seen someone use words to damage, hurt, and tear others down. Give an example of how we can use words to bless, build up, and strengthen others.

10. "Authority takers" shut people down, discourage them, and cause them to dream less. How should we respond when we are in relationship with an authority taker? How do we keep from being discouraged and shut down by people like this?

11. What is a step you can take in the coming week to give God more complete authority over your life? Why is this challenging for you and how can your group members pray for you as you seek to submit this area of your life to God?

Whether you're an authority taker or your life is surrounded by authority takers, it's critical to begin changing your environment and seeing yourself through God's eyes.

## Closing Prayer

*Spend time in your group praying in some of the following directions:*

- Thank God for creating the world as a beautiful place for us to live and follow Him.
- Pray for wisdom to see how you can care for creation and be attentive to your responsibility to steward this planet.
- Thank God for the people He has put in your life and pray that you will grow in your ability to nurture, encourage, and help them follow God more closely.
- Ask God to help you use your words to build others up and encourage them.
- Pray that people will mirror God more clearly because they have been around you.

> When you call on Jesus's name in prayer, you're accessing His authority for the purpose of fulfilling His plan in your life.

## Looking in the Mirror

*Take time to engage in one or more of the following exercises before your next group meeting.*

### 1. Environment Creators

God has given you authority and filled you with His strength so that you can actively work at creating environments and settings where the people around you can thrive, grow, and follow God's purposes and plan for their lives. Choose two or more of the areas of life, or relationships, listed below and write down some specific ways you can make this environment more conducive to glorifying God and helping people grow in their faith:

### In a close friendship

Ways I can intentionally shape this environment to help others pursue God's purposes and grow in their relationship with Jesus:

•

•

•

### In my workplace

Ways I can intentionally shape this environment to help others pursue God's purposes and grow in their relationship with Jesus:

•

•

•

**In my church**

Ways I can intentionally shape this environment to help others pursue God's purposes and grow in their relationship with Jesus:

- 

- 

- 

---

The most powerful expression of authority given to the church is to create an environment that brings people into the presence of God.

---

**In a marriage**

Ways I can intentionally shape this environment to help others pursue God's purposes and grow in their relationship with Jesus:

- 

- 

-

### With my children
Ways I can intentionally shape this environment to help others pursue God's purposes and grow in their relationship with Jesus:

- 

- 

- 

### With my extended family
Ways I can intentionally shape this environment to help others pursue God's purposes and grow in their relationship with Jesus:

- 

- 

- 

### In a social setting I am part of on a regular basis
Ways I can intentionally shape this environment to help others pursue God's purposes and grow in their relationship with Jesus:

- 

- 

-

**In my neighborhood**

Ways I can intentionally shape this environment to help others pursue God's purposes and grow in their relationship with Jesus:

- 

- 

- 

Make a point of putting a couple of these into action in the coming days. As you do this, pray that God will use you to reflect His image as you seek to create places where others encounter Jesus, grow in faith, and pursue His will for their lives.

### 2. Stewards of Creation

God has made a wonderful place for us to live, an environment where we can thrive, grow, and follow Him. Make a list of three things you can do in your home, workplace, church, neighborhood, or some other setting that will lead to good stewardship of this world.

- 

- 

- 

Make a point of acting on one or more of these goals in the coming week. As you do, take time to prayerfully thank God for making such a magnificent place for us to live. Also, invite the Holy Spirit to convict you any time you are not being a good steward of creation.

---

The Holy Spirit prompts us to pray
for the purpose of glorifying God.

---

### 3. Building and Blessing

Write down the names of four people in your life whom you care
about. Under their name, write two specific things about them that
you can bless, praise, or affirm:

**Person:**
A word of blessing I can share—

A word of blessing I can share—

**Person:**
A word of blessing I can share—

A word of blessing I can share—

**Person:**
A word of blessing I can share—

A word of blessing I can share—

**Person:**
A word of blessing I can share—

A word of blessing I can share—

Take time in the coming week to share a word of encouragement and affirmation with at least two people on this list. You can send an email, a handwritten letter, or a tweet, call them on the phone, videoconference with them, or even talk face-to-face.

### 4. Journal . . .

*Use the space provided below to write some reflections on the following topics:*

- Ways I see God using the authority He has given me to create places where others can pursue Him and grow in faith.
- My observations of how I see God present in creation and how I am feeling compelled to care for and exercise humble authority as I grow as a steward of His beautiful world.
- How are you doing in your effort to speak words of blessing to others? How are others using their words to encourage and build you up?
- How do the people in my life experience or perceive me?
- How do people mirror God more because they are in relationship with me?

## Recommended Reading

In preparation for session 5, you may want to read part 4, chapters 13–16, of the book *God in the Mirror*.

# You Were Created to Be
# GOD'S FRIEND

## Introduction

Have you ever been hurt by a friend? The truth is, we all have!

Sally is a seven-year-old who tells her best friend that she is afraid of spiders. It seems silly, but the very thought of spiders kind of freaks her out. Two days later three boys on the playground decide to chase Sally around while holding little spiders and threatening to put them in her hair. As she runs and cries for help, she sees her best friend laughing and realizes that she has betrayed her trust and told the boys about her secret fear. At seven years old, Sally learns that trust is a fragile thing and she begins to guard her heart.

Ricardo has a circle of high school friends and he is thankful that he has a sense of belonging to a group that gets along and watches each other's backs. For the first time he feels like he is on the "inside" of a relational group that really matters to him. Then, on a Thursday night he goes out to get a burger at a local spot and sees the whole group of guys hanging out, eating, and laughing. As he sits in his car looking in the window at everyone in the group (except him), he checks his phone for texts, a call, or some sign that he was invited and just missed it. Ricardo drives off without a burger and wondering if his friends are still his friends. One moment, a shadow of doubt, and trust can begin to erode.

Stan and Phyllis have been tight friends with the Taylors for a number of years. They have made a point of spending three to five days vacationing together for the past four summers. They love this time of fun, friendship, and connecting. Now it is June and nothing is planned for the summer. Stan and Phyllis drop a few subtle hints that they have some open time in July and August, but the Taylors don't bite. In a conversation in the privacy of their own home, Stan and Phyllis wonder out loud as a couple, "Did we do something wrong? Have we offended our friends? What happened?"

We can be seven or seventy and face the same realities. Relationships can be fragile. Trust can easily be broken. Friendships are a gift, but they don't always last and endure. Through all of this we can find ourselves protecting our hearts and avoiding the relational intimacy we crave and need. If we are not careful, these same attitudes of caution can impact the way we connect with God.

## Talk about It

What are some of the qualities of a good friend?

Tell about a good friend you had in your childhood, during your teenage years, or as an adult. What does it take to build a healthy friendship?

---

You were created to know and love God, to be His image bearer and His friend.

---

**Video Teaching Notes**

*As you watch the DVD teaching segment for session 5, use the following outline to record anything that stands out to you, or simply use the bullet points as reminders of what Miles talked about in this session.*

- Satan's plan: destroy your relationship with God

- God's eternal relationship in the Trinity

- Love that extends to the people around us glorifies God

- Right brain, left brain, and learning to trust

---

No one in this life will compare
with the friendship Jesus offers
to you—not your brother, your
spouse, your cousin, your
mamma, your daddy, no one.

---

## DVD Discussion

1. Tell about a time that you experienced a breech in trust in a friendship or close relationship (without using a specific name). How did this experience impact your trust level and how you look at relationships in general?

**Read** Genesis 3:1–13 and Job 1:6–12

2. What tactics does Satan use to try to damage our relationship with God and trust in God?

When we fall for these tactics, how does this impact our relationship with God and with other people?

3. How can we actively fight against these same tactics today and seek to stay in close relationship with God and the people He has placed in our lives?

---

Satan knows that your God image is powerless outside of a dependent relationship with your heavenly Father.

---

**Read** Genesis 2:15–25

4. How does God feel about people being alone? What does this passage reveal about God's plan, design, and dream for the people He has made?

---

If we're going to live in relationship with God as His friend, we must also live in relationship with His family, the global church.

---

**Read** Matthew 22:34–40

5. What are the two greatest commandments God has placed before His people? What do these have in common? What can we do to live out each of these commandments?

6. In the video, Miles emphasizes the idea that if we live outside of relationships, we can't do the two things that God says matter most in the entire world. What is he getting at? Why is a close and intimate relationship with God essential to live a life of vibrant faith?

Why are good friendships with the people around us essential for becoming the people God wants us to be?

7. What are tactics and ways Satan tries to destroy our friendships with the people in our lives who really matter?

Which of these has the enemy been using on you and how can you battle back against this attack?

**Read** John 17:20–26

8. God not only models community and friendship within the Trinity, but He calls His people to build healthy and honoring friendships with each other. What are some of the results that come when Christians learn to love each other and have healthy relationships?

What are some possible consequences if we live with open conflict and broken relationships with other Christians?

---

Every Christian in the
world is your relative.

---

9. Miles teaches that our relationship with God and even with other people begin and end with trusting in God. He emphasizes that good relationships are based on our confidence that God is faithful and trustworthy. How do you respond to this idea?

How does deep and abiding trust in the faithfulness of God help us build healthy relationships with the people in our life?

The more we sacrifice on behalf of others, the more pure and evident is our friendship with Christ.

10. What erodes and damages your trust in God and, as a result, your trust in people? Why is it important to be honest about this?

11. What helps you live and walk with an enduring trust in the faithfulness of God? How can you deepen your trust level?

## Closing Prayer

*Spend time in your group praying in some of the following directions:*

- Thank God that He wants to be your friend and praise Him for what He has done in Jesus to make friendship with you a possibility.
- Pray that you will be a great friend to the people God has placed in your life.
- Praise God for His amazing example of relational harmony in the Trinity.

- Ask the Holy Spirit to help you notice and battle against the tactics of Satan as he tries to ruin your relationship with God and the people in your life.
- Pray for eyes to notice people around you who feel relationally disconnected and ask God to help you be a bridge builder for those who feel left out.
- Invite the Holy Spirit to heal the places in your heart where you still carry scars of relational hurt.
- Pray that you will learn to be a friend of God on a deeper level and that this spiritual reality will flood into the rest of your relational world.

> The evidence of our friendship with God is our changed lives.

## Looking in the Mirror

*Take time to engage in one or more of the following exercises before your next group meeting.*

### 1. Celebrating Friendships

Plan a gathering of some friends whom you have not connected with recently. Make it fun and substantial. Bring these people together with three things in mind:

- To enjoy friendship and the gift of relationships. Make sure there is space for laughter and play!
- To express what these people mean to you. Take time to let each person know, in an open time of affirmation, or in private

conversations, how much they mean to you. Express your appreciation to each person.

- To give God glory. Take time, as you are together, to pray and lift up expressions of thanks and praise to God for these people. Tell God what you appreciate about your friends and praise Him for giving you the gift of friendship. If you want to go one step deeper, you might want to read portions of John 17 (Jesus's prayer) and let these friends know how you see God making this prayer a reality as you share life together in Christ-honoring Christian friendships.

### 2. Healing Hearts and Building Bridges

Take time to reflect back through your relational life. Identify two or three times when trust was broken or a friendship was damaged because of something you did or said. That's right, don't focus on how someone else hurt you, but invite the Holy Spirit to search your heart and show you where your harsh words, neglect, or actions broke trust and hurt a person in your life. You might want to read and reflect on Psalm 139:1–4, 23–24 in this process.

Try to identify two or three situations you have faced and write down what comes to your heart:

1. A person that I may have hurt: _____
   The situation:

What I said or did (or failed to do):

What I could have done better:

What I could do today to restore trust and reveal God's faithfulness in my relationship with this person:

2. A person whom I may have hurt: _____
   The situation:

What I said or did (or failed to do):

What I could have done better:

What I could do today to restore trust and reveal God's faithfulness in my relationship with this person:

3. A person whom I may have hurt: _____
   The situation:

What I said or did (or failed to do):

What I could have done better:

What I could do today to restore trust and reveal God's faith-fulness in my relationship with this person:

Pray about contacting at least one of these people and taking action (one of the ideas you wrote down above) that will build trust, restore the friendship, honor God, and be a blessing to this person.

---

God speaks the truth. He speaks the
words your spirit needs to hear.

---

### 3. Making Time for Your Friend

A friendship with God takes time and needs investment of more than an hour on Sunday. Sometimes a friendship falls into disrepair simply because we don't invest the time needed to nurture intimacy. Walk through the simple steps below in an effort to develop a more disciplined rhythm of time with God.

- Review the past seven days (look at your schedule if needed). How much time did you set aside to be with God, to worship Him, to read His Word, to talk with Him in prayer, to serve Him, and to grow your friendship. Be honest about this and write down what you learn:

**Time I spent with God over the past week:**

| Day: | Time: | How I connected with God as a friend: |
|---|---|---|
| Day: | Time: | How I connected with God as a friend: |
| Day: | Time: | How I connected with God as a friend: |
| Day: | Time: | How I connected with God as a friend: |
| Day: | Time: | How I connected with God as a friend: |
| Day: | Time: | How I connected with God as a friend: |
| Day: | Time: | How I connected with God as a friend: |

- Reflection on my time with God. As I look over the past several days, here is what I notice . . .

How much time I really spend connecting with God and growing this wonderful relationship—

When I do spend time with God, I tend to spend it doing the following—

One aspect of my friendship with God I noticed was missing (or not very deep) was—

- I want to grow my friendship with God by taking some steps forward. How can I invest more time in this friendship? What will I do to make my time with God rich, meaningful, and alive? Three ideas—

  1)

  2)

  3)

- Make time in the coming week to add in more time with God and to try one of the ideas above. Then, in two weeks, walk through this process again!

---

You'll never be loved as deeply and perfectly as God loves you.

You'll never be more safe and secure than in His care.

You'll never be more YOU than when you are His friend.

---

*4. Journal . . .*

*Use the space provided below to write some reflections on the following topics:*

- Write down some of the ways you see the enemy trying to damage your friendship with God.
- Make a list of ways you see Satan trying to harm your friendships with other followers of Jesus.
- Make notes of some of the ways you are growing in love with God and with the people in your life.
- Journal some thoughts on how you can deepen your friendship with Jesus.
- Keep a list of various ways you see God reaching out to you as a loved friend.
- Write down some of the ways God has proven Himself trustworthy and faithful.

_____

_____

_____

_____

_____

_____

_____

_____

_____

_____

_____

_____

_____

_____

_____

## Recommended Reading

In preparation for session 6, you may want to read part 5, chapters 17–20, of the book _God in the Mirror_.

Session 6

# You Were Created to Be
# ETERNAL

## Introduction

Let's be honest. Our perspective on heaven, eternity, and the greatness of God is limited. Because our daily lives are fixated on jobs, schedules, meal preparation, doctors' visits, shopping, and many other mundane responsibilities, we simply can't see the bigness of God and eternity from where we stand.

The story is told of a little boy sitting and talking to his grandpa about big topics like God, time, and eternity. The boy asked, "Grandpa, how long is a thousand years to God?" His grandpa answered, "It is like a second" as he snapped his fingers.

The boy reflected a moment and asked, "How much is a million dollars to God?" "I guess it is like a penny," said the grandpa. The boy pondered what his grandpa had said as he went on with his day.

That night, as he went to bed, the boy decided to pray about some of the things he had learned from his grandpa. He asked, "God, is a million dollars just like a penny to You?" He heard God say, "Why, yes it is!" So the boy smiled and boldly asked, "Dear God, would You be willing to give me a penny?" God responded just as quickly, with a divine smile, and said, "I would be glad to, and I'll give it to you in just a second!"

## Talk about It

When you think of heaven and eternity, what pictures and ideas come to your mind?

Why is it important for Christians to reflect on eternity and remember that every person we meet is an eternal being?

---

You were not created to die.
You were created to live forever.
Where will your forever be?

---

 ## Video Teaching Notes

*As you watch the DVD teaching segment for session 6, use the following outline to record anything that stands out to you, or simply use the bullet points as reminders of what Miles talked about in this session.*

- How do you picture you and God?

- Keeping our eyes fixed on what matters most

- You are **Individually Unique**

- You are God's **Moral Mirror**

- You are given **Authority to Rule**

- You are **God's Friend**

- You are **Eternal**

---

You are going to live
forever somewhere.

---

## DVD Discussion

1. If you were going to draw a picture of you and God together, and give it to God so He could look at it and see how you perceive your relationship with Him, what would this picture look like?

**Read** 1 John 3:1–3

2. What do you learn about yourself, now and in eternity, from this passage?

When you read "We shall be like him," what do you think this means?

---

Since eternity is forever,
it has already begun.

---

**Read** John 14:2–4; Colossians 3:1–7; Revelation 7:13–17; 21:4–7; and 22:3–6

   3. What does the Bible teach us about heaven? What pictures, images, and ideas does God use to help us get a grasp of something our minds can't fully comprehend?

**Read** Luke 16:19–31; Matthew 13:36–43; and Revelation 21:8

   4. What does the Bible teach us about hell? What pictures, images, and ideas does God use to help us get a grasp of something our minds can't fully comprehend?

---

Hell is the place where every good
thing associated with God is absent.

---

**Read** Colossians 3:1–4 and Hebrews 12:1–3

   5. What do these passages teach us about where we should keep our mind, eyes, and the focus of our lives? What warnings does the Bible give about letting our eyes and minds wander toward unhealthy things?

What are one or two "earthly things" you feel God wants you to spend less time focusing on? What steps can you take to shift your mind and life away from these things?

---

Good actions replace bad
thoughts with good thoughts.

---

6. In the video Miles challenges us to aspire to become the person we will be in eternity. In other words, don't wait until heaven, but strive for it now! If you were seriously committed to become who you will be in eternity today, how might this change *one* of the following areas of your life:

How you view and use your finances . . .

How you spend your free time . . .

How you serve those who are in need . . .

How you share the love and message of Jesus with others . . .

How you work and behave on the job and at school . . .

Some other area of your life and walk with Jesus . . .

7. You are made to mirror the image of God and that means you are **Individually Unique.** Miles encourages us to beware that we don't become a counterfeit version, a knockoff, of what God really wants us to be. What are some of the ways we miss God's best for us when we fail to become the individually unique person God has designed us to be?

**Read** Leviticus 11:44–45 and 1 Peter 1:13–16

8. You are made to reflect the image of God and that means you are made to be a **Moral Mirror** of God in this world. Miles gives a challenge for us to do all we can to reflect a clearer picture of God in our life every day, starting today! Take a moment and write a sentence or two in response to each statement below:

*One way I can grow in holiness and reflect God's perfect and pure presence in my life is:*

*One way I can be more honest with my friends and family is:*

*I could love my enemy more by:*

*When it comes to my sexuality, I could honor God with greater purity in my body and mind by:*

*I could show God's love to my spouse with greater consistency if I would:*

*My words would honor God more and bless others with greater frequency if I would stop:*

*My words would honor God more and bless others with greater frequency if I would begin to:*

*My intimacy with Jesus would increase if I would take time, every day, to:*

After you have written your own reflections, share one of these with your group and invite them to pray for you as you seek to reflect God with greater clarity in the moral mirror of your life.

9. You are made to reflect the image of God and that means you are given **Authority to Rule**. When God placed Adam and Eve in the garden, He gave them authority to rule in a way that would be productive and God-honoring. In eternity we will still have responsibility to use authority in a way that pleases God. How can you develop and exercise humble and God-honoring authority in *one* of the ways listed below?

In how I conduct myself in the workplace . . .

In how I treat my spouse . . .

In how I lead and invest my life in my children . . .

In how I serve and lead in my church . . .

In how I use my influence in my community . . .

In some other area of my life . . .

**Read** John 17:20–26

    10. You are made to reflect the image of God and that means you are made to be **God's Friend.** What kind of relationship does Jesus pray you will have with God and with the people in your life? What is one step you can take, this week, to grow your friendship with God and how can your group members encourage you and keep you accountable as you take this step?

**Read** Philippians 3:13–16

    11. You are made to reflect the image of God and that means you are **Eternal.** Miles talks about his time in the NFL and reflects on the reality that he had to deny himself (his desires and wants) many times so that he could stay in shape to compete on the field. What is something you need to deny or refuse (sometimes over and over) so that you can keep getting ready for heaven and reflect the eternal God with greater clarity in your life?

God created us as eternal spiritual
beings so we could communicate
and have a relationship with
an eternal spiritual God.

## Closing Prayer

*Spend time in your group praying in some of the following directions:*

- Ask God to help your life reflect Him more and more with each passing day.
- Ask the Holy Spirit of God to help paint healthy and biblical pictures in your mind of God and yourself.
- Thank God that heaven awaits you, through faith in Jesus, and pray that you will live each day with a confident certainty of your eternal destiny.
- Invite God to use you to share the lifesaving, good news of Jesus, with people who are still wandering far from Him. Pray that they will follow Jesus and be with Him in heaven someday.
- Ask the Spirit to show you where your eyes have wandered and are not on Jesus the way they should be.
- Pray for your eyes, mind, and heart to be fixed firmly on God at all times.

---

When you pray, you are reaching into the unseen eternal world. Prayer is communication with an eternal God.

---

## Looking in the Mirror

*Take time to engage in one or more of the following exercises.*

## 1. Draw a Picture

Use the space below to draw two different pictures of you and God together. You can use a pencil, pen, or even colored Crayolas.

**PICTURE 1**—How I saw God in relationship to me when I was very young (or a young Christian, or even at the beginning of this small group experience):

**PICTURE 2**—How I see God in relationship to me today:

*Share these pictures with a Christian friend and talk about how your view and picture of God has grown and matured as you have learned more about what the Bible teaches about who God is. Also, share about how your view of yourself has developed and grown through the six weeks of this group study.*

---

You were created to know God's
love and live in His glorious
presence all your life.

---

## 2. Training Plan

Miles talks about the tough reality that self-denial and discipline are part of the growth process that makes us more like Jesus. Just like an athlete eats well, says no to unhealthy foods, and works out relentlessly, we will need to train ourselves as we move toward eternity.

Take time to write down some of the things you can begin doing, and stop doing, that will help you train for eternity. Use the prompts below to guide you.

I can prepare for eternity and reflect God more clearly in the mirror of my life if I will **begin** . . .

Goal in my family life—

Goal in my workplace—

Goal with my neighbors—

Goal in my church—

Goal in some other area of my life—

I can prepare for eternity and reflect God more clearly in the mirror of my life if I will **stop** (or cut back on) . . .

Goal in my family life—

Goal in my workplace—

Goal with my neighbors—

Goal in my church—

Goal in some other area of my life—

---

The more sacrifice, surrender,
and worship you give to God,
the more you glorify Him.

---

### 3. Focus Experiment

One of the ways we prepare for eternity is learning to keep our hearts and eyes on Jesus. The more we see, study, and reflect on who He is, the more we can become like Him. Pick a day in the coming week and try this little experiment: Set a timer to ring or vibrate once every hour throughout the day. When it rings, read or reflect on Colossians 3:1–4 and Hebrews 12:1–3. If you have a phone that can do it, have these passages pop up as your alarm notification.

With these prompts, take a few minutes every hour and ask this question: *How can I keep my mind and eyes on Jesus during this portion of my day?* Pray for your mind to stay focused on Jesus in growing measure.

At the end of the day, write down a few thoughts and observations in response to the questions below:

- What drew my eyes and heart from Jesus as I walked through the day?

- What helped me keep my mind and eyes on Jesus?

- How can I develop triggers throughout my day to get my focus back on God and His will for my day?

---

My prayer is that you'll allow Jesus
to fill your heart like a hand in a
glove so you can live the rest of
your life to its fullest potential.

---

*4. Journal . . .*

*Use the space provided below to write some reflections on the following topics:*

- How I am learning to keep my eyes and heart focused on Jesus.
- New images and understandings of who God is.
- Fresh new outlook on who God wants me to be.
- Prayers I am lifting up for people in my life who need to enter a lifesaving relationship with Jesus.
- How I am seeing God shine His image through me to the lives of the people I encounter each day.
- Ways I want to grow in holiness and mature in faith.

_____

_____

_____

_____

_____

_____

_____

_____

_____

_____

_____

_____

_____

_____

_____

_____

_____

_____

## Recommended Reading

As a review, you may want to read any portions of the book *God in the Mirror* that you have not yet read.

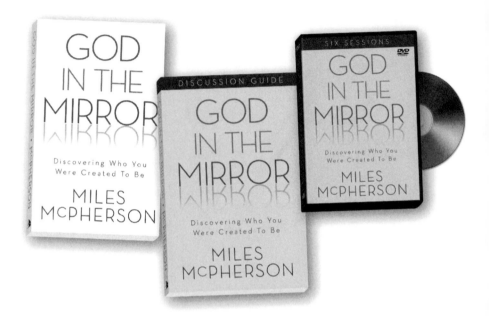

# Connect with
# Miles McPherson!

Known for his frank and funny delivery, Miles loves to call people to think about how God has prepared them to do something significant with their lives. He's a prolific speaker, one who can talk to anyone — from prison inmates to senior citizens. He challenges everyone to go out and do something for God!

## Visit
# WWW.MILESMCPHERSON.COM

- Check out Miles' blog
- Watch Rock Church Live online
- Stay informed with Miles' e-newsletter
- Plus much more . . .

 @milesmcpherson | pastor.miles.mcpherson